Quiz Show

Alice Leonhardt
Illustrated by Carl Salter

Rigby

A Harcourt Achieve Imprint

www.Rigby.com
1-800-531-5015

Plains

Elementary
Fifth Grade Team

Plains Member 1

Plains Member 2

Quiz Show Host

Plains Member 3

Plains Member 4

Stewart

Elementary
Fifth Grade Team

Leon

Stacey

Ms. Jung, Stewart
Elementary
School teacher

Raja

Patricia

Act I

Scene 1

Narrator: The big Quiz Show match between rival teams from Stewart Elementary School and Plains Elementary School is about to begin.

Leon: We've got to do our best today if we want to win and go on to the final match next month.

Stacey: I'm nervous because I've heard that Plains Elementary is a tough team to beat.

Raja: I don't think we'll have a problem beating the Plains team because we've been practicing, and we know our material.

Stacey: Charlotte really knows her geography material, and I hope she gets here soon because we need her if we want to win this one.

Narrator: Ms. Jung, a teacher at Stewart School and coach for the Quiz Show team, comes into the room.

Ms. Jung: Good morning! I'm glad you're all here, but I have some bad news about Charlotte. She has the flu, and she won't be able to be in today's game.

Raja: Oh no, Charlotte is our best team member!

Stacey: Charlotte answers all of those difficult geography questions about cities and countries all over the world, and nobody is as smart as she!

Ms. Jung: Don't worry, because I have asked someone to take Charlotte's place. I would like you all to meet Patricia Fuentes, who is a new student from California.

Narrator: Patricia smiles at the team as Ms. Jung helps her sign in, and the other team members start to worry about the game.

Scene 2

Narrator: Round one of the game is about to begin, but without Charlotte, things look tough for the Stewart Team.

Raja: I don't know why Ms. Jung thinks that Charlotte can be replaced.

Leon: Adding a new team member at this late time will never work!

Plains Member 1: Hey, we heard that one of your team members, Charlotte, has the flu.

Plains Member 2: Yes, isn't she the one on your team who knows the most about geography?

Leon: Yes, but the rest of us know geography, too, so we will be fine.

Narrator: Patricia comes back and joins the group, but she doesn't say anything.

Stacey: I wish that I had worked harder on those geography questions, instead of relying on Charlotte to know all of the answers.

Patricia: I really like geography, and it was my favorite subject at my school in California.

Raja: OK, then tell me where the city of Rome is located.

Patricia: Rome is the capital of Italy, which is in Europe.

Leon: Maybe we have a chance after all!

Act II

Narrator: Everyone in the room gets quiet as the Quiz Show host comes out on stage to begin the match.

Quiz Show Host: The rules are that I'll go back and forth between the two teams, asking each team member a question. A correct answer by one of the team members scores one point, but if someone misses a question, the opposing team gets a chance to answer it correctly. If they answer it correctly, they get a point.

Quiz Show Host: Spelling is the subject for round one, and the first word goes to the Plains Team, so please spell the word *business*.

Plains Member 3: *Business* is spelled b-u-s-i-n-e-s-s.

Quiz Show Host: That is correct. Stewart Team, please spell the word *cousins*.

Stacey: *Cousins* is spelled c-u-s-i-n-s.

Quiz Show Host: I'm sorry, but that spelling is incorrect. Can someone from Plains Team spell the word *cousins* correctly?

Plains Member 2: The word is spelled c-o-u-s-i-n-s.

Quiz Show Host: That is correct, Plains Team, so now you must spell the word *fraction*.

Plains Member 4: The word is spelled f-r-a-c-t-i-o-n.

Quiz Show Host: Correct again! Stewart Team, your next word is *confusion*.

Leon: *Confusion* is spelled c-o-n-f-u-t-i-o-n.

Quiz Show Host: I'm sorry, that is an incorrect spelling. Plains Team, please try to spell the word *confusion*.

Plains Member 1: It is spelled c-o-n-f-u-s-i-o-n.

Narrator: The spelling round continues, but things aren't looking good for the Stewart Team, and at the end of round one, the score is Plains Team 6, Stewart Team 1.

Quiz Show Host: The subject for the second round is "people in history," and this time we'll start with the Stewart Team. We all know that George Washington was our first president, but who was the second president of the United States?

Stacey: We just learned this in class, so I know that the second president of the United States was John Adams.

Quiz Show Host: You are correct. Now Plains Team, please name one president who appears on Mount Rushmore in South Dakota.

Plains Member 1: Thomas Jefferson is one of the presidents who appears on Mount Rushmore.

Plains

Quiz Show Host: That's correct. Stewart Team, who was president of the United States when the American Civil War began?

Leon: Was it Abraham Lincoln?

Quiz Show Host: Yes, that's correct. Plains Team, please tell us who invented the lightbulb.

Plains Member 4: Um, I think it was Benjamin Franklin who invented the lightbulb.

Quiz Show Host: I'm sorry, but that is incorrect, so can a team member from Stewart answer this question?

Patricia: I think that it was Thomas Edison.

Quiz Show Host: Yes, Thomas Edison is the correct answer!

Narrator: Things are going better for the Stewart Team, but at the end of the round, the Plains Team is still leading by a score of 11 to 5. The teams are taking a break before they begin round three.

Act III

Scene 1

Raja: I don't think that we've ever been this far behind in points before.

Leon: Geography, the hardest subject, is coming up, and we won't win the game unless we answer all of our questions correctly in the next round.

Narrator: Ms. Jung, carrying a stack of books, comes to cheer on the team during their break.

Ms. Jung: Why do I see such gloomy faces on this team? You did well in round two, and you'll do even better in the last round if you use your break time wisely.

Stacey: We shouldn't even bother looking at those geography books because Charlotte was our geography expert, and we barely have a chance of winning without her.

Patricia: I know that I'm just a beginner and that all of you have been in thousands of these games, but maybe Ms. Jung is right. I'm sure we can do really well in round three if we work just a little harder.

Leon: You mean if we work *a lot* harder.

Patricia: OK, if we work *a lot* harder, but you're a great team, so anything is possible. When Ms. Jung picked me to be on the team, I was so excited.

Stacey: You really wanted to join the team even though you were new to the school?

Patricia: Yes, when I first came here, I watched you compete against Handley Elementary, and you were very good! I remember thinking how great it would be if I could be on your team.

Raja: Patricia's right about that match being great. We were one point behind, and Leon and Charlotte answered those really hard math questions.

Patricia: You're a strong team, so I'm sure you can win again!

Stacey, Raja, Leon: She's right, we *all* can do it!

Scene 2

Narrator: It is time for the final round, and everyone is wondering how the Stewart Team will do.

Quiz Show Host: The subject for the final round is geography, and we will begin with the Stewart Team. Please name one South American country located south of the equator.

Raja: Argentina is in South America and is located south of the equator.

Quiz Show Host: That's correct. Plains Team, on what continent would you find the countries France and Spain?

Plains Member 1: France and Spain are on the continent of Europe.

Quiz Show Host: You're right! Stewart Team, in what state is the volcano Mount St. Helens located?

ARGENTINA

Stewart

Leon: Mount St. Helens is in the state of Washington.

Quiz Show Host: That's correct! Plains Team, where would you find Mount McKinley, the highest mountain in North America?

Plains Member 2: Um, is it in Colorado?

Quiz Show Host: That's incorrect. Stewart Team, do you know the answer?

Stacey: Yes, Mount McKinley is located in Alaska!

Quiz Show Host: Alaska is the correct answer!

Narrator: Stewart is doing so well that at the end of round three the score is tied 14 to 14!

Quiz Show Host: OK, it's time for a geography question that will break the tie! I have one more really hard question left, and the team that answers it first will win today's match!

Narrator: Both teams think that they will win. Everyone can feel the excitement in the air.

Raja: We tied the Plains Team, and we can do this, too!

Stacey: But it's going to be a *really* hard question, so let's listen carefully.

Leon: Then we'll just have to think *really, really* hard!

Quiz Show Host: Here is the final question: Where are the Marias Islands located?

29

Narrator: All of the team members, except Patricia, stare at the host, trying to think where this unfamiliar place might be.

Quiz Show Host: Can anyone answer the question?

Patricia: I can because I once visited the Marias Islands, which are three islands located off the coast of Mexico.

Narrator: Members of the Stewart team look back at the host, holding their breath, wondering if Patricia gave the right answer.

Quiz Show Host: That is correct! Stewart Elementary is the winner of this Quiz Show!

Raja: We won, thanks to Patricia!

Stewart

31

Stacey: Not only did you answer the question to break the tie, Patricia, you helped us to believe that we could do really well today.

Leon: For that you should get all of the medals, and we hope you'll get to be a part of the team again.

Narrator: Patricia's teammates place all four medals around her neck as they enjoy their success.

Raja, Leon, Stacey, Patricia: Three cheers for the Stewart Team! Next stop is the final match in Dallas, Texas!